ORCA
FOOT...

Microbes to the Rescue

USING BACTERIA, ALGAE AND FUNGI
TO CLEAN UP THE PLANET

YOLANDA RIDGE

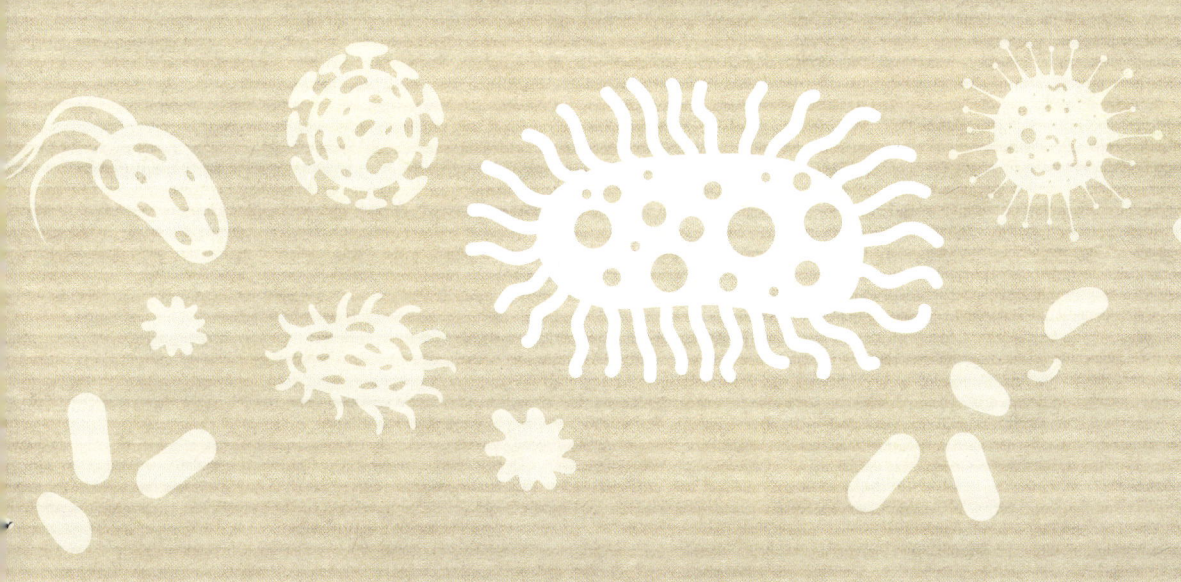

ORCA BOOK PUBLISHERS

Text copyright © Yolanda Ridge 2025

Published in Canada and the United States
in 2025 by Orca Book Publishers.
orcabook.com

All rights are reserved, including those for text and data mining, AI training and similar technologies. No part of this publication may be reproduced or transmitted in any form or by any means, electronic or mechanical, including photocopying, recording or by any information storage and retrieval system now known or to be invented, without permission in writing from the publisher. The publisher expressly prohibits the use of this work in connection with the development of any software program, including, without limitation, training a machine-learning or generative artificial intelligence (AI) system.

Library and Archives Canada Cataloguing in Publication

Title: Microbes to the rescue : using bacteria, algae and fungi to clean up the planet / Yolanda Ridge.
Names: Ridge, Yolanda, 1973- author.
Series: Orca footprints ; 34.
Description: Series statement: Orca footprints ; 34 | Includes bibliographical references and index.
Identifiers: Canadiana (print) 20240387759 | Canadiana (ebook) 20240387767 | ISBN 9781459839137 (hardcover) | ISBN 9781459839144 (PDF) | ISBN 9781459839151 (EPUB)
Subjects: LCSH: Microbiology—Juvenile literature. | LCSH: Microbial biotechnology—Juvenile literature. | LCSH: Microorganisms—Juvenile literature. | LCSH: Environmental protection—Juvenile literature. | LCSH: Nature—Effect of human beings on—Juvenile literature. | LCGFT: Informational works. | LCGFT: Instructional and educational works.
Classification: LCC QR57 .R53 2025 | DDC j579—dc23

Library of Congress Control Number: 2024939274

Summary: Part of the nonfiction Orca Footprints series for middle-grade readers and illustrated with color photographs throughout, this book explores how microbes can help address some of the most pressing environmental challenges on Earth.

Orca Book Publishers is committed to reducing the consumption of nonrenewable resources in the production of our books. We make every effort to use materials that support a sustainable future.

Orca Book Publishers gratefully acknowledges the support for its publishing programs provided by the following agencies: the Government of Canada, the Canada Council for the Arts and the Province of British Columbia through the BC Arts Council and the Book Publishing Tax Credit.

The author and publisher have made every effort to ensure that the information in this book was correct at the time of publication. The author and publisher do not assume any liability for any loss, damage, or disruption caused by errors or omissions. Every effort has been made to trace copyright holders and to obtain their permission for the use of copyrighted material. The publisher apologizes for any errors or omissions and would be grateful if notified of any corrections that should be incorporated in future reprints or editions of this book.

Front cover photos by Manjurul/Getty Images, AndreasReh/Getty Images and monkeybusinessimages/Getty Images.
Back cover photos by Orla/Getty Images, gorodenkoff/Getty Images and Glenn Price/Shutterstock.com.

Design by Dahlia Yuen.
Edited by Kirstie Hudson.

Printed and bound in South Korea.

28 27 26 25 • 1 2 3 4

Microbiologists are scientists who study the behavior, growth and interaction of microbes.
SOLSKIN/GETTY IMAGES

This book is dedicated to microbes and the scientists who study them.

Contents

Introduction 7

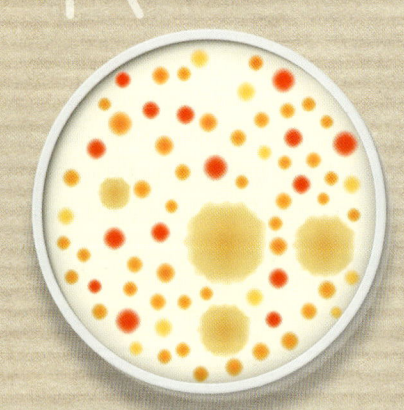

CHAPTER ONE
TACKLING POLLUTION

Agricultural Runoff 9
    Mycomania 10
    Fungi Sponges 11
Dealing with Disaster 12
    Oil Spills 12
    Nuclear Distaster 14
Try This! Grow Your Own Mycelium 16

CHAPTER TWO
THE PLASTIC PROBLEM

Plastic-Eating Bacteria 19
    Learning to Love It 20
    Enzyme Action 20
Bioplastic 21
    Petroplastic 22
    Edible Packaging 22
    Flip Flops and Surfboards 23
Try This! Build a Microcomposter 25

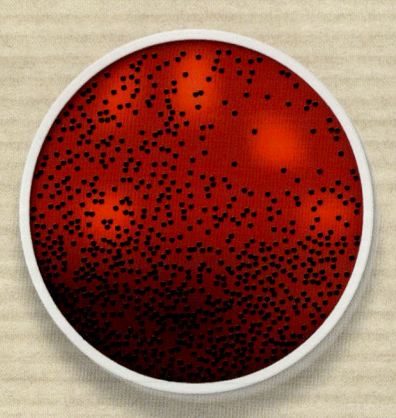

CHAPTER THREE
FOODS OF THE FUTURE

Sustainable Agriculture 27
    Three Sisters 29
    Building the Microbiome 30
Eating Differently 31
    Farm-Free Food 32
    Spirulina 33
Try This! Make Focaccia for Dinner 36

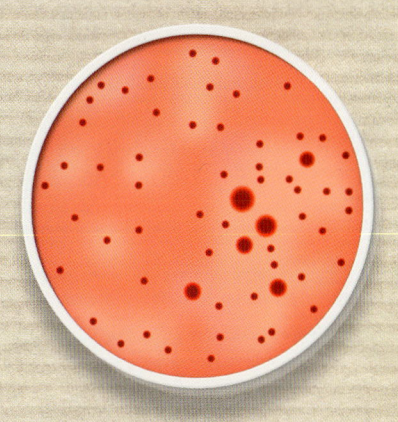

CHAPTER FOUR
ENERGIZING EARTH

Carbon Capture 39
    Mycorrhizal Networks 40
    Algae Meets AI 41
Mighty Microbes 42
    Algae Fuel 42
    Electromicrobiology 43
    The Microbial Revolution 44
Try This! Create an Algae Bioreactor 46

Acknowledgments 47
Resources 48
Glossary 49
Index 51

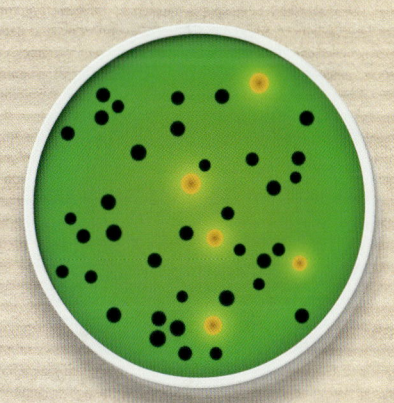

What Is a Microbe?

A microbe is an *organism* that can only be seen with a microscope. Since *micro* means "extremely small," microbes are also called microorganisms. Bacteria, fungi and algae are three different types of microbes.

Microscopic organisms can't be seen unless they're magnified through the lens of a microscope.
DEMAERRE/GETTY IMAGES

Introduction

Can microbes help clean up the planet? They may be small, but they're mighty. Plus, there are billions of them! And they're everywhere!

Left alone, microbes such as bacteria, fungi and algae are experts at adapting, surviving and thriving under extreme and constantly changing conditions. They capture *carbon*, eat plastic, break down pollutants and contain energy that can be transformed into fuel. Engineered by scientists, these microbe superpowers can be maximized to benefit the *ecosystem* they're part of while providing people with things like food and electricity.

To save the planet from *pollution* and the effects of the *climate crisis*, and to create a sustainable future, we need to find alternative and inventive solutions. Let's explore how microbes can shrink our environmental footprint through the production of things like eco-friendly packaging and farm-free food. To get a sense of their power, we'll also dig into activities that show microbes at work. There are downsides to relying too much on bug-based technologies, however, which we'll uncover in the Under the Microscope section of each chapter.

Let's get buggy!

CHAPTER ONE

Tackling Pollution

We all know pollution is bad. What many of us don't realize is how much of it is produced by the things we make, grow and use every day.

Let's take jeans as an example. Every pair starts as a cotton plant, typically grown using *fertilizers* and *pesticides* that get washed into rivers, lakes and groundwater. Once harvested, cotton goes to a factory where it's dyed and made into fabric, using chemicals that further pollute both the water and air. Jeans ready for market are packaged in plastic for shipping and selling. If no one buys them—or they go out of fashion—they end up in the garbage and become land pollution.

Water, air and land pollution, all from just one pair of jeans! And that doesn't even include the pollution produced by generating energy for everything from fueling the jean-making machines to transporting materials from farm to factory to store.

Instead of feeling guilty about the pollution created by what's in our closets—we all have to wear something!—we're going to focus on ways of making the process less harmful, and on how microbes can help.

Every year, close to five billion pairs of jeans are sold around the world.
TENDO23/GETTY IMAGES

The jeans in your closet start as cotton plants that are harvested, dyed and processed into fabric.
(MAIN) LUCAS NINNO/GETTY IMAGES; (INSET) ESIN DENIZ/GETTY IMAGES

AGRICULTURAL RUNOFF

When fertilizers and pesticides build up in the soil and are washed into the environment, they cause natural ecosystems to get out of balance. This agricultural runoff doesn't only happen with cotton-growing. It happens with most things grown on a large scale, making agricultural runoff one of the top three sources of pollution in rivers, streams, lakes, wetlands and oceans.

It's a big problem, but, luckily, lots of little microbes can make it smaller. Let's start by focusing on a microbe that's a bit easier to see than the others. In fact, you may have seen some on your walk to school—clinging to the bark of a tree or hiding out in the shade of a bush. How can fungi get rid of pesticides and fertilizers in agricultural runoff? By sucking them up like a sponge!

Many, Many Microbes!

There are many different species within categories of living things like bacteria, algae and fungi. There are probably a lot of microbes that scientists haven't even found yet—especially bacteria.

Group	Number of Species
Bacteria	> 1,000,000,000
Algae	27,000
Fungi	144,000

Mycelium can be tiny, forming a colony that's too small to see without a microscope. It can also be large enough to cover an entire forest.
TAVIPHOTO/SHUTTERSTOCK.COM

Mycomania

Before you start picturing tiny, mushroom-shaped sponges, we need to talk about mycelium. The fungus most of us are familiar with is the cap and stem of a mushroom. But all fungi—including the mushrooms on your pizza—grow from mycelium. Usually found underground, mycelium is a collection of microbes that suck nutrients out of the soil or tree or whatever **organic matter** the fungi's growing on (and it can grow on some pretty gross stuff!). All fungi have mycelium, but not all mycelia have fungi, kind of like how all flowers have a plant but not all plants have a flower.

Mycologists (scientists who study fungi) refer to a lot of fungi-related things with the prefix *myco* (including themselves!). So it probably won't surprise you that using mycelium to reverse environmental damage caused by pollution is called **mycoremediation**. What might surprise you is all the different ways mycoremediation can be used.

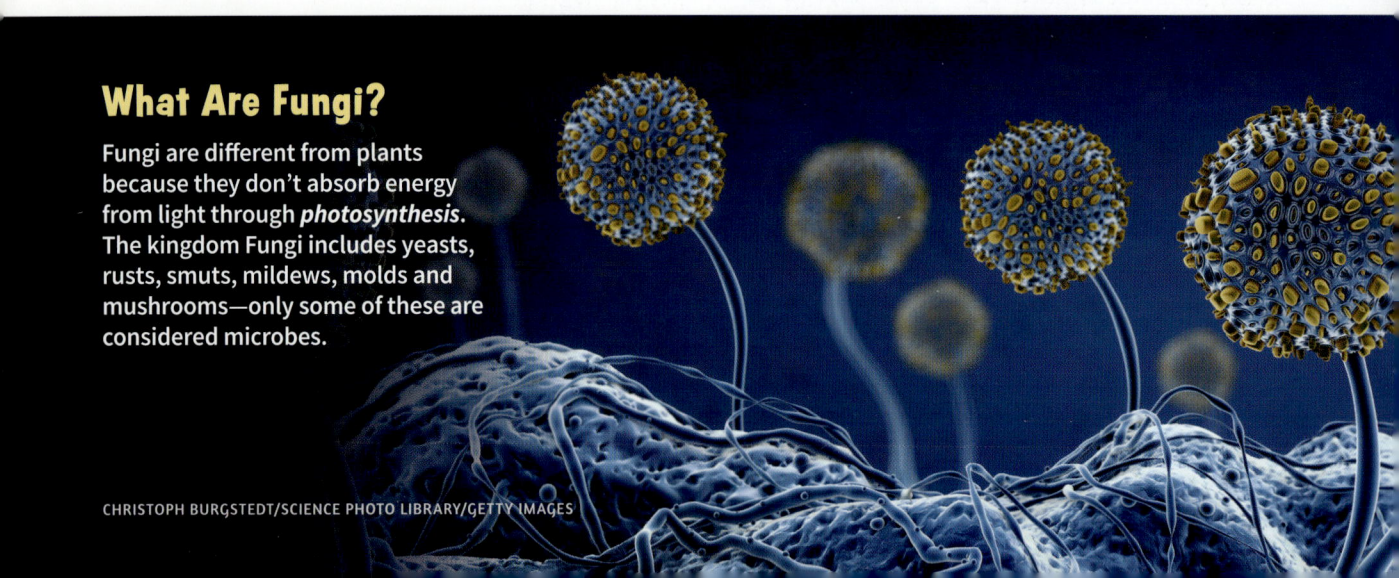

What Are Fungi?

Fungi are different from plants because they don't absorb energy from light through *photosynthesis*. The kingdom Fungi includes yeasts, rusts, smuts, mildews, molds and mushrooms—only some of these are considered microbes.

CHRISTOPH BURGSTEDT/SCIENCE PHOTO LIBRARY/GETTY IMAGES

Mushroom Dress

Mycelium is often described as threadlike and fibrous. Could that be how fashion designer Aniela Hoitink got the idea to use it to make clothing? She started by creating a new mycelium fabric called MYCOTEX. From this success, Hoitink and her team figured out how to grow mycelium in circular pieces that could be molded over a body form to make a dress—no sewing required! Her company's focused on fashion, but other inventors have made everything from faux leather to chairs to doors out of mycelium.

ANIELA HOITINK, MYCOTEX

Fungi Sponges

It's a little unclear who first thought of throwing a bag of mushrooms into polluted water to sponge up the mess. Whether it was a formally trained mycologist or someone learning from information passed down through generations, the result was somewhat miraculous. It turns out that passing water through a web of mycelium can remove both pesticides and fertilizers.

The process is known as mycofiltration (there's that prefix again!) and it's being studied by mycologists as a new method of cleaning up polluted water. How well it works depends on the type of pollutant and what method is used. It's a bit like choosing whether you need a mop, broom or vacuum to clean up a mess in the kitchen.

Studies have shown that mycoremediation does a pretty good job of removing stuff like copper, zinc, iron, cadmium, lead and nickel. In addition to agricultural runoff, fungi sponges can soak up **synthetic** chemicals used to turn raw materials like cotton into fabric. In fact, microbes can be used to clean up a lot of the toxic material created in mining and the manufacturing of everything from jeans to computers to cars. Going beyond fungi sponges, matching the right microbe to the right pollutant gives us the best chance of sopping up the mess.

Passing water through a filter can separate microscopic particles.
DAVID H. COLLIER/GETTY IMAGES

DEALING WITH DISASTER

Okay, so what about the energy required to run all these farms, factories and mines? Until recently most of it's come from burning **fossil fuels** or from **nuclear power plants**. Both have downsides—especially fossil fuels (which we'll talk more about later)—and people around the world are working hard to capture energy from renewable and sustainable sources such as solar and wind power instead. In the meantime, our fungi friends and their mycelium have helped us clean up a few big messes resulting from past power production, such as oil spills and nuclear disaster.

Oil Spills

Fungi microbes are the star of the Amazon Mycorenewal Project, which aims to clean up a horrible mess in Ecuador, a country in South America. Over a 20-year period, about 18 billion gallons (68 billion liters) of waste—enough to fill more than 27 thousand Olympic-sized swimming pools—was released in a remote area of the jungle by a company extracting oil from the ground.

Oil contains many different compounds that are harmful to plants and animals. Microbes can help make these compounds less toxic.
KIRILL GORSHKOV/GETTY IMAGES

Oil spills happen all over the world. This New Zealand beach is being cleaned by volunteers after it was polluted by oil from a container ship that ran aground.
STEVE CLANCY PHOTOGRAPHY/GETTY IMAGES

Some of it went directly into rivers and streams that more than 30,000 people depend on for drinking, cooking, bathing and fishing. Other waste—crude oil and toxic sludge—was poured directly into pits that still smell like a gas station many years later and look like pools of thick, black tar.

With input from the five Indigenous communities that live in the area, international groups have tried to mop up the oil spills in different ways. One method uses burlap bags filled with:

- Cardboard
- Sawdust
- Wood chips
- Straw

Microscopic mycelium is added to the bags before they are placed in the pools of oil. Once wet, the mycelium has all it needs to grow. As it grows on the organic matter, it also breaks down the oily sludge underneath, turning the toxins into something less harmful.

It's not much harder than throwing a bag of mushrooms into polluted water, but the Amazon Mycorenewal Project has improved water quality and sponged up some of the mess. Things will probably never be the same in this part of Ecuador, however, which is partly why oil companies have been forced to clean up their act. Members of the nonprofit group that started the project are still hard at work, teaching and supporting locals. They're also applying what they've learned to other cleanup efforts, such as fixing soil pollution caused by wildfires.

Burlap bags sponge up polluted water. Mycelium growing inside the bags breaks down toxic compounds.
(MAIN) JOHN ELK III/GETTY IMAGES; (INSET) LJUPCO SMOKOVSKI/SHUTTERSTOCK.COM

Radioactive waste spread across Europe after the Chernobyl disaster. Pollution created by the nuclear-reactor explosion is still present in the area around the power plant almost 40 years later.
LUX3000/SHUTTERSTOCK.COM

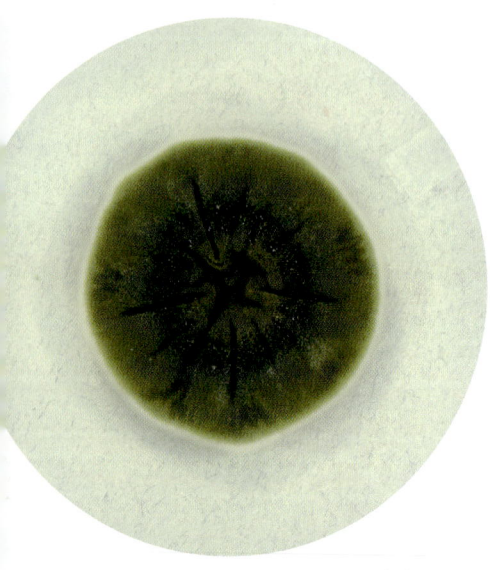

Radiotrophic fungi growing around the Chernobyl nuclear power station is often referred to as "black mold."
MEDMYCO/WIKIMEDIA COMMONS/CC BY-SA 4.0

Nuclear Disaster

From cotton fields to oil spills, we've come a long way with using mycelium, and it's just one of many microbes! Before we dig into the power of tinier bugs, though, let's talk about fungi as the hero of another disaster. One of the biggest environmental accidents in the world is the nuclear meltdown that happened at Chernobyl nuclear power station in 1986. When part of the power plant exploded, ionizing *radiation*—particles charged with so much energy that they're toxic—polluted the area. More than 360,000 people had to move away, and many others became sick from radiation poisoning after the disaster.

It's still not safe for people to live in an area of Ukraine around Chernobyl, but one thing that does live there is—you guessed it—fungi. Since the discovery of one fungus species growing on the walls of the nuclear reactor, others have been identified and added to a group of organisms called radiotrophic fungi. All radiotrophic fungi have one thing in common—they feed off ionizing radiation. Most also contain a substance called melanin—the same thing that gives color to our eyes, hair and skin. Because of this, scientists believe it's the melanin in the mycelia that allows radiotrophic fungi to get the energy they need to grow from ionizing radiation.

Knowing about the connection between melanin and radiation is an important step in being able to isolate the active ingredient and concentrate it for use (kind of like figuring out what specific vitamins you need rather than taking a daily multivitamin). Beyond cleaning up after nuclear disaster, scientists have figured out how to combine melanin with other things to protect humans from radiation when they travel to space. And because these fungi grow from ionizing radiation, they could even become the perfect crop for producing a totally different type of fuel, for feeding astronauts.

Under the Microscope
Too Good to Be True?

From agricultural runoff to nuclear disaster, mycoremediation seems to be a good alternative to current methods of cleaning up water and land pollution, which tend to use harsh chemicals, heat and lots of energy. But are mycofiltration and mycorenewal too good to be true?

In general, fungi's an inexpensive, energy-efficient way to tackle pollution, using nature to restore healthy ecosystems. We do have to be careful about introducing mushrooms to areas they don't normally grow, however. If too many mushrooms grow too fast, they can become an *invasive species* that can throw ecosystems out of balance in totally different ways.

The other potential downside to mycoremediation is it generally takes a lot of time—often years or even decades. We need to figure out how to make the process more efficient, through things like matching specific mushrooms to specific pollutants, for example. Active ingredients in mycelium can also be isolated and concentrated, but this must be done through careful scientific study. We don't want dinner-plate-sized mushrooms becoming pollution themselves!

Fungi grow in a large range of habitats. Most mushroom species prefer damp, dark environments.
LANDONPARENTEAU/PIXABAY.COM

Try This! GROW YOUR OWN MYCELIUM

If you've never seen mycelium growing underground, this is the experiment for you. You'll be surprised how fast it grows!

Materials:

- A sealable glass container
- Corrugated cardboard
- Oyster mushrooms
- A small knife

Method:

1. Cut cardboard to fit the container.
2. Soak cardboard in water for 20–30 minutes, until the layers can be separated easily (you may have to weigh the cardboard down with something heavy).
3. Drain and separate the layers (you should have some that are corrugated or wavy and some that are flat).
4. Cut tiny slices off the stem of the mushroom, starting at the bottom.
5. Put a corrugated sheet of cardboard in the bottom of the container.
6. Add slices of mushroom evenly and fairly close together.
7. Put another layer of cardboard on top and add more mushroom slices.
8. Continue to layer, using only corrugated cardboard or alternating between corrugated and flat, until container is full or mushroom slices are gone.
9. Close the container with a lid and store in a dark place at room temperature.
10. Open container every day to make sure it stays fresh and moist (you may need to spray water into the container once in a while) and check on the mycelium growth.

After a few days, the mycelium will start to appear through the edges of the cardboard. Over time it will seep through the cardboard, filling in all the gaps and holes.

Looking for ideas on what to do with your mycelium crop? Try growing some on an old pair of jeans! All you need to do is wet the jeans, spread a bit of mycelium, roll them up tight and put them in a plastic bag or enclosed container with a few holes. Keep the jeans moist at room temperature, and you should have new oyster mushrooms in a couple weeks. Bon appétit!

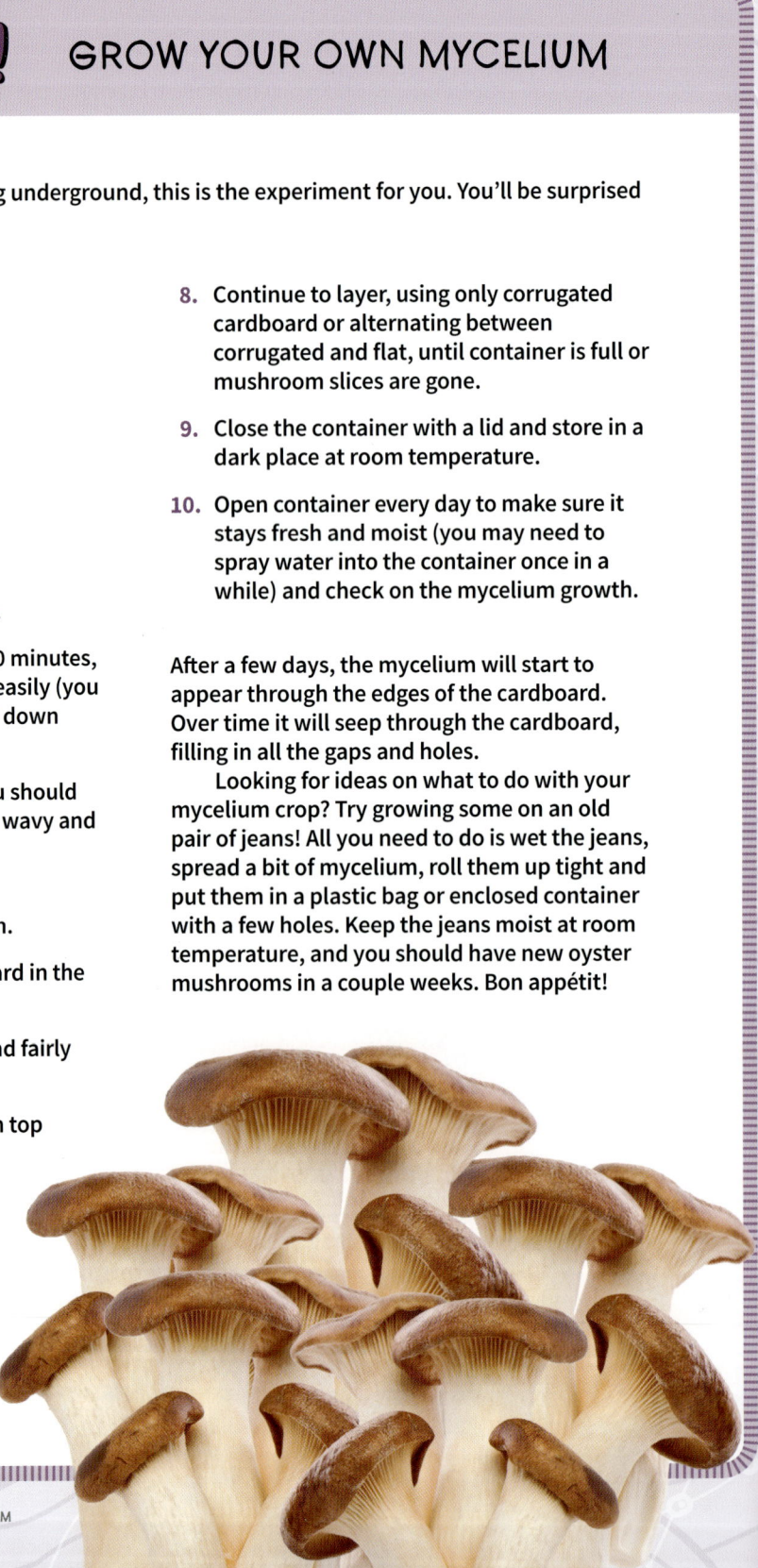

GLENN PRICE/SHUTTERSTOCK.COM

YOLANDA RIDGE

YOLANDA RIDGE

YOLANDA RIDGE

17

CHAPTER TWO

The Plastic Problem

Composting is the natural process of recycling organic matter into nutrient-rich soil.
RENATA ANGERAMI/GETTY IMAGES

Fungi aren't the only microbes that can turn pollutants into something less toxic. The ability of microbes to break stuff down into smaller pieces is the magic behind composting. You put a pile of food scraps together, and microbes decompose it into nutrient-rich soil. Microbes like fungi and bacteria feed off organic matter, whether it's in our compost pile or in the natural environment. Even those jeans "no longer fit to be worn in public" (according to your mom, anyway!) will be broken down in a landfill. The fabric's **biodegradable** because it's made of organic matter. Yep, those jeans started as a cotton plant, and like any plant that's put in the compost pile, they will eventually decompose.

There are a lot of things microbes have a hard time breaking down, though, and that includes human-made materials like plastic. That's why dealing with plastic is difficult—it sticks around for a long time and doesn't decay or decompose, even after we're done with it.

Most plastic is nonbiodegradable because very few microbes can break it down.
CASTKA/GETTY IMAGES

PLASTIC-EATING BACTERIA

As a biology student at Reed College in Portland, Oregon, Morgan Vague knew all about the importance—and limitations—of microbes when it comes to decomposing pollution. So imagine her surprise when she found bacteria that could break down plastic.

Vague isolated the bacteria from samples of dirt, sand and water she collected in an area of Texas with a large amount of oil pollution. With over 300 different strains of bacteria in these samples, how do you think she found the one that could live off plastic? By giving them only one thing to eat. That's right—plastic! Bacteria that couldn't break it down died. The ones that could grew into colonies with the potential to help humanity with our plastic problem.

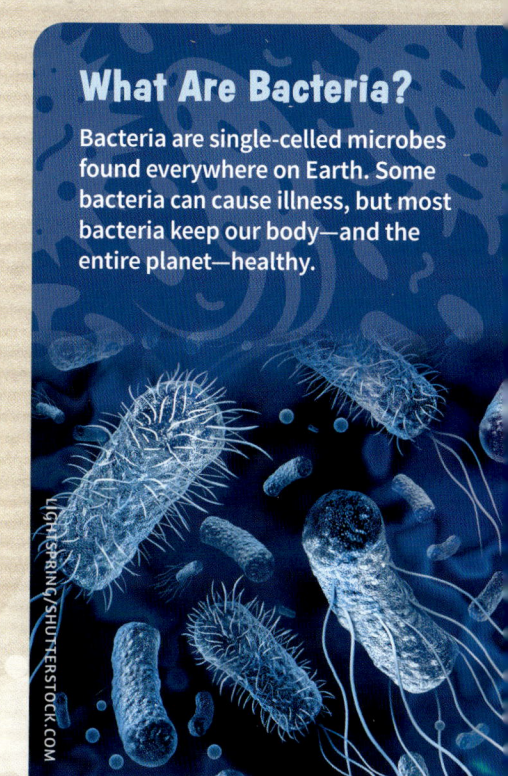

What Are Bacteria?

Bacteria are single-celled microbes found everywhere on Earth. Some bacteria can cause illness, but most bacteria keep our body—and the entire planet—healthy.

LIGHTSPRING/SHUTTERSTOCK.COM

May Contain Plastic?

It's obvious that some things contain plastic, like single-use containers, toys and garbage bins. But plastic (especially microplastic) is also hidden in some not-so-obvious places, such as:
- Fleece clothing
- Chewing gum
- Glitter
- Produce stickers
- Sunscreen

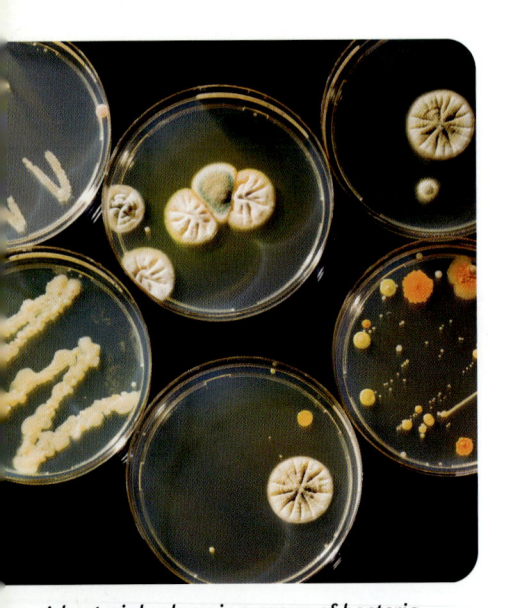

A bacterial colony is a group of bacteria derived from the same mother cell.
WLADIMIR BULGAR/SCIENCE PHOTO LIBRARY/ GETTY IMAGES

Learning to Love It

Given how much plastic is in our environment, it's not surprising that microbes have learned to love it—that's why Vague was looking for them in the first place. And she wasn't the first researcher to discover plastic-eating bacteria. The thing about bacteria is that they grow and divide quickly, which means they can adapt and *evolve* quickly in response to their environment. If they're given only plastic to eat, changes in the *genome* of some lucky bacteria will allow them to eat just that. Various types of plastic-eating bacteria have been identified by Vague's team and other scientists around the world. Unfortunately, none of them can tackle the plastic crisis alone—there's just too much of it. That's why scientists are working on ways to make bacteria more efficient.

Enzyme Action

There are a couple of different ways scientists can make plastic-eating bacteria better at turning plastic into dirt. One is to isolate the *enzyme* in bacteria that actually does the work of breaking down plastic. Once isolated, the enzyme can then be mass-produced or combined with others to create a super-enzyme with super plastic-eating potential. Identifying specific enzymes is also what researchers try to do when they find mycelium that can break down certain toxins, like the melanin we talked about in chapter 1.

Another option is to speed up the evolution of different plastic-eating bacterial strains so they can chomp through various types of plastic much faster and survive warmer temperatures. The eventual goal is to develop a super-enzyme or superbug that can be used to break down plastic in landfills and recycling facilities. Some scientists are also trying to produce a formula that could be sprayed on the mountains of plastic polluting our oceans, waterways and other natural ecosystems.

Algae live in both fresh and salt water.
JABILTON/GETTY IMAGES

VIDEOLOGIA/GETTY IMAGES

BIOPLASTIC

There's a different approach to the plastic problem, of course, and that's to stop using so much nonbiodegradable plastic in the first place! This is where another microbe enters the picture—algae. Have you ever been to a pond in the late summer and seen green slime floating on the water? That pond scum is algae, one of the oldest forms of life on the planet and an important part of a healthy ecosystem—as long as there's not too much of it.

To understand how pond scum can turn into plastic, it helps to know a bit more about where plastic comes from. Don't worry—this isn't about the birds and the bees (not at the reproductive level, anyway). It's about polymers.

What Is Algae?

Most algae live in water and make their own food through photosynthesis. They're different from plants because they don't have stems or leaves, and they don't produce flowers or seeds.

Small plastic granules are the building blocks of objects such as bottles, packaging and electronic components. HEMANTPHOTOGRAPHER/GETTY IMAGES

Bioplastic created with microbes can be used to make takeout food containers that decompose. KALI9/GETTY IMAGES

Petroplastic

All plastics are polymers, which means they're made up of building blocks that are linked together to make a chain. Different types of plastic are made from different building blocks. The plastics most commonly used today are made of chemical polymers that come from **petroleum**, the type of oil extracted from the ground in places like Ecuador and Texas.

Petroplastic is cheap to produce, lightweight but strong and can be molded into almost any shape. Because it's such a convenient way for people to package, preserve and produce stuff, the discovery of petroplastic changed human life.

The downside to petroplastic is one we already talked about—it doesn't biodegrade. Some of it breaks down into microplastics, which are harmful to the environment and the animals that live in it (including us!). This has led scientists and inventors to look for alternatives in some of the most unlikely places—like the pond.

Edible Packaging

What makes algae a good alternative to petroplastic? First, algae contains a compound also found in petroleum, so it can be used to produce similar polymers with the same advantages as petroplastic. Second, it grows quickly in small spaces using less water than land plants while still taking **carbon dioxide** out of the air—something that also helps with the climate crisis.

To turn seaweed—a not-so-microscopic algae—into bioplastic, researchers follow a simple three-step process:

1. Dry   2. Grind   3. Shape

Using a special machine, this type of bioplastic can be turned into packaging or used to create things you might not even think of as being plastic, like the shiny coating on your takeout container that stops the grease from soaking into the cardboard.

Containers made of seaweed, for things such as ketchup and salad dressing, are naturally broken down by microbes.
BRENT DURAND/GETTY IMAGES

One company has taken this idea to the next level by producing seaweed containers for sauces and drinks that can be consumed along with what's inside. If the idea of eating the wrapper leaves a bad taste in your mouth (even though it's designed to be tasteless), no problem—plastic made from seaweed is fully biodegradable. Nature can make it disappear pretty fast, as it's been breaking down algae for millions of years.

Flip-Flops and Surfboards

Microscopic algae, too, can be used to make bioplastics. Since it's a bit more difficult to harvest in the wild compared to larger algae species like seaweed and kelp, most bioplastic producers grow microalgae in human-made ponds or **bioreactors**. When it's ready, they extract it and make a paste. The oily part is then separated out to create a biofoam that's used to make things like flip-flops and surfboards.

Wait. Foam? Yes, foam's a plastic too—it's just softer and more airy than the plastic in your AirPods. Harder plastics like that are also being created out of algae polymers that can be used in **3D printing**. By isolating different parts of an algae **cell**, scientists are working to make all sorts of bioplastics that are as versatile and convenient as petroplastic.

(FLIP-FLOPS) SERHII TSYHANOK/SHUTTERSTOCK.COM; (SURFBOARDS) STEVE HEAP/SHUTTERSTOCK.COM

Under the Microscope
Too Good to Be True?

The world is slowly moving away from plastic products, especially single-use items like straws and grocery bags. Bioplastic might be a good alternative to petroplastic, but we probably don't want to rely on it too much. Even if the plastic is biodegradable, the world can only handle so much of it. And with a growing population, our best option is to use and buy less stuff.

We also need to use caution when growing algae, as it can become a type of pollution when it grows out of control. This happens when there are extra nutrients in the water. Too much of a good thing—like nitrogen and phosphorus, minerals often used on farms as fertilizer—can cause algae blooms. Beaches and swimming areas are sometimes shut down because of the toxins produced by algae blooms. But they don't just put people at risk. Algae blooms also make life difficult for things living under them, because they block out sunlight.

It's important to make sure that a super-enzyme or superbug can be sprayed on piles of plastic without any negative consequences. What if it breaks the plastic down into something even worse? Or what if the microbe evolves further into something we can't control? Ongoing research is required to make sure we don't create an even bigger mess trying to clean up the one we've already made.

Algae blooms form when there are excess nutrients in the water, warmer temperatures, extra light and stable wind conditions.
MICHAEL G. MILL/SHUTTERSTOCK.COM

Try This! BUILD A MICROCOMPOSTER

You might already have a composter in your backyard. With this countertop version, you can see the microbes at work.

Materials:

- A large glass jar such as a mason jar or empty pickle jar
- Shredded newspaper or cut-up cardboard (such as half an egg carton, one empty paper-towel tube or two empty toilet-paper tubes)
- A big handful of dirt
- A small handful of dried leaves
- A variety of vegetable and fruit scraps (such as peels and cores)
- A half cup water

Method:

1. Put newspaper/cardboard, dirt, leaves and food scraps in jar or bottle.
2. Stir or shake (with lid on) until combined.
3. Add water and stir or shake again. If mixture looks dry, add up to a half cup more water.
4. Cover opening with a kitchen towel or paper towel secured with elastic. If you prefer to use the jar lid, punch holes in it so the compost will still get some air circulation.
5. Check daily to make sure it stays moist (you may need to add a few spoonfuls of water, if it's warm).

It will take about four weeks for the mixture to fully decompose, but after a week you should start to see it breaking down. The smaller the food scraps, the faster you will see results (pro tip: help your microbial pals by snipping banana peels and other large scraps into pieces with scissors).

You can experiment with adding other kitchen scraps, like coffee grounds and clean eggshells, but never add dairy or animal products, because they get stinky and attract pests. Once your compost looks like soil, use it to pot a plant or grow a seed (see chapter 4).

CRYSTAL BOLIN PHOTOGRAPHY/GETTY IMAGES

CHAPTER THREE

Foods of the Future

Water-containing microbes can be used to grow plants without soil.
PIRANKA/GETTY IMAGES

Edible packaging may be part of the solution to limiting pollution. But what about the food inside? Can microbes be used to help us eat in a way that's better for the planet too?

In the first chapter we talked about agricultural runoff, pollution that comes from growing food on a large scale. Grains, vegetables and fruit grown with fertilizers and pesticides all produce agricultural runoff. It's also created by the animals we farm for food because guess what cows, pigs and chicken eat? Often the same things as we do—especially grains like wheat and vegetables like corn—grown in ways that can be bad for the environment.

As the human population expands, we'll need more crops and livestock to feed all the hungry people and animals. The development of synthetic pesticides and fertilizers allowed us to keep up with the growing demand for food in the past.

But knowing about their negative effects on ecosystems, we can't just keep using more of them. That's why some scientists are turning to microbes for help.

Cow farts contain methane gas, a byproduct of microbes breaking down the food the cows eat.
ANDRESR/GETTY IMAGES

SUSTAINABLE AGRICULTURE

By now it's probably clear to you that microbes are powerful. Because of their superpowers, scientists love to isolate specific microbes to better understand what they're doing and how they're doing it. But in nature, microbes live in a community with other microbes. A sample of soil from your backyard, community garden or local playground contains millions of microbes—mostly bacteria and microscopic fungi.

Carrots grow by absorbing nutrients provided by microbes in the soil.
YUJI SAKAI/GETTY IMAGES

You already know what they're doing there—making the soil healthy through decomposition—and they do this dirty work as a team. When we introduce chemical fertilizers and pesticides, it can make plants healthy in the short term, but it makes this community—or **microbiome**—unhealthy in the long term, kind of like having too many chefs and not enough dishwashers.

Researchers are learning a lot about microbiomes. For example, the microbiome of the soil in which your carrots grew will affect the microbiome of your gut. Yep, that's right! Microbes are just as important to our bodies as they are to the soil. And they're helpful in the same way, too, because they break down food and extract nutrients as part of the digestive process (and they're responsible for the loud burp you made after dinner!).

Three Sisters

Farmers have understood the importance of soil microbiomes for centuries. They didn't have to look at dirt under a microscope to know that some plants grow better together than others. Why? Because different plants attract different microbes, so the soil's microbiome changes based on what's growing in it.

Sounds good, but what does it have to do with sisters? Haudenosaunee and Anishnaabe First Nations first referred to corn, beans and squash as the three sisters. When planted together, these vegetables support each other's growth while limiting weeds and pests. How? The most obvious answer is because of what happens above the soil. For example, corn provides a strong stalk for pole beans to grow up, and squash leaves shade the ground and prevent the soil from drying out.

Below the soil, there's a lot more going on. Bean plants—like their cousin the pea—are basically nitrogen-fertilizer factories. We're not talking about a factory full of machines producing chemicals that can be sprayed on the field. It's a specific type of bacteria that does all the hard work by taking nitrogen out of the air and making it available to the plants. The bean-plant roots, in turn, provide the bacteria with a nice home in which to live and grow. Thanks to this *symbiotic* relationship between microbe and plant, synthetic fertilizers containing nitrogen aren't necessary. This results in less soil and water pollution—a win for farmers, plants and the environment!

Corn, bean and squash plants grow well together.
PHOTOHAMPSTER/GETTY IMAGES

Rhizobia bacteria grow in nodules around plant roots, where they help capture and deliver nutrients.
STDOUT/WIKIMEDIA COMMONS/CC BY-SA 3.0

Liang Cheng used common ragweed as a model plant for his research.
COURTESY OF LIANG CHENG

Building the Microbiome

In the lab, scientists use this type of wisdom to perfect soil microbiomes based on things like climate and what farmers are hoping to grow—or not grow. As a horticulture student at Cornell University, Liang Cheng researched which microbiomes can help one plant grow while limiting the growth of others. The right microbiome can reduce the use of pesticides by discouraging weeds and invasive plants. It's like throwing a party and serving the food and drink that your friends like but your enemies don't.

Cheng used his microbe knowledge as a member of the Cornell Weed Team. You read that right—a weed team! Around the world, teams like Liang's compete in contests to identify weeds and come up with new and inventive ways to stop them from limiting the growth of plants that farmers (and consumers) want in their fields.

In many parts of the world, we can buy whatever food we want whenever we want it. This puts a lot of pressure on farmers, the environment and microbes!
THAI LIANG LIM/GETTY IMAGES

EATING DIFFERENTLY

The other way of increasing food production without increasing pollution is to change what we eat. Corn, beans and squash are all good—and there are lots of other "sisters" that grow well together—but in many parts of the world, people have become used to going to the grocery store and buying whatever they want at a reasonable cost. This puts a lot of pressure on farmers, especially as growing conditions change because of the climate crisis.

I'm not going to suggest we start eating dirt instead of bananas, but what about going directly for a helping of microbes? You've probably been warned that bacteria's bad for you—that's why you have to wash your fruits and vegetables and be very careful about handling things like raw chicken. But even though there are some "bad" bacteria, there are also some "good" ones. For example the ones in soil that help plants grow, and the ones in your stomach that help you grow. So why not use bacteria to bypass the farm all together?

Germs and Bugs

Not all microbes make you sick. The ones that do are referred to as germs or bugs.

31

Farm-Free Food

Here's a recipe developed by researchers in Finland to do just that:

1. Mix bacteria, water and carbon dioxide together in a bioreactor.
2. Use a jolt of electricity to split water molecules into hydrogen and oxygen.
3. Add carbon dioxide, along with a dash of ammonia, phosphorus and salt.
4. Give the bacteria time to chomp down the hydrogen.
5. Process into protein powder.

The result may not sound that appetizing, but it could be used to feed livestock or maybe even become a meat alternative for us (not such a far-fetched idea for those of us who already put protein powder in our smoothies). The goal behind formulas this like is to produce food using fewer resources and creating less pollution. But what about places where food can't grow at all? Microbe-based foods could also become part of the menu for astronauts living in space (served with a side of radiation-grown fungi!).

It's not as futuristic as it sounds. So many scientists and companies are using bacteria, fungi and yeast to create microbial protein that some people predict there will be a microbial food revolution. Other people compare these meat alternatives to processed foods (which are often less healthy because of added salt, sugar and fat) and prefer the idea of returning to more traditional methods of farming. Unfortunately, that kind of farming requires more fertile land at a time when there's less of it due to population growth and the climate crisis. Fortunately, there's a microbe that can grow almost anywhere that's been used as a food source for hundreds of years: pond scum.

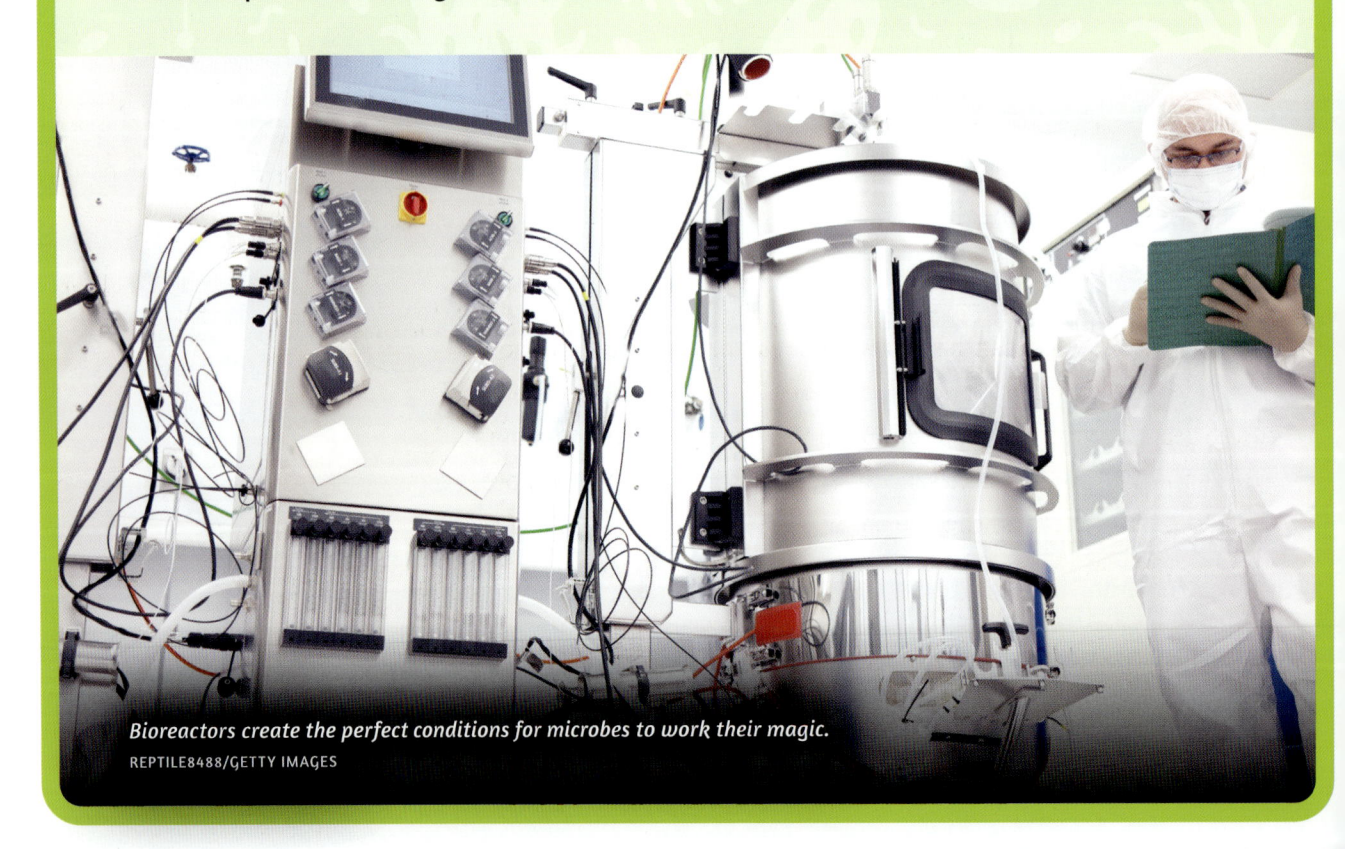

Bioreactors create the perfect conditions for microbes to work their magic.
REPTILE8488/GETTY IMAGES

Spirulina

Okay, so pond scum is unlikely to make it onto the menu of a high-end restaurant. But did you know that one of the most popular supplements in the world is a type of microscopic blue-green algae? Taken as a dark-green powder or a tablet, spirulina is highly nutritious and a great source of protein, copper and B vitamins. It has other potential health benefits as well and became popular in recent years when NASA suggested it could be grown in outer space as a superfood for—you guessed it—astronauts!

Blue-green algae can be grown in fresh or salt water without pesticides or fertilizers. A company that gives people with limited resources a new way to generate income has been helping farmers grow spirulina in countries such as Thailand, India and Singapore. Instead of bioreactors, they've found ways to grow the algae in unique and unused spots like hotel rooftops. This is especially important in parts of the world where space is limited and conventional crops are becoming harder to grow because of hotter, drier and stormier weather caused by the climate crisis.

Spirulina is microscopic algae that some people consider a superfood.
(MAIN) MARCINWOJC/SHUTTERSTOCK.COM;
(INSET) ANASTASIA KOROVINA/GETTY IMAGES

Under the Microscope
Too Good to Be True?

Eating microbes can be a hard concept for people to swallow! But the way we feed ourselves today—with food produced using lots of land, water, pesticides and fertilizers—is not a sustainable option in a future with more people and a changing climate. Microbial proteins are a good alternative as long as the formula for making them doesn't require too much energy or other resources. Microbes might not need a farm to grow, but energy is required to cool, heat and stir bioreactors. The microbes themselves also have to be cultivated and fed with something like hydrogen or sugar.

It's also important that we don't accidently create microbes that grow so well they become another invasive species. Some people are also concerned about changing the genome of a bacterial or algae cell through *gene editing*. Most of us eat genetically modified food already—and scientific studies show it is not a risk to human health—but caution is still required when messing with microbial genes.

Another concern is that many people could lose their jobs in a farm-free future. Not just farmers but people who make everything from tractors to pesticides to seeds. New jobs would be created, though, such as metabolic engineers, computational biologists, lab assistants and nutritionists.

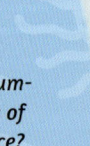

Mission specialist Leland Melvin surrounded by vacuum-packed food on the orbiter Atlantis. Could astronauts of the future eat microbial-based food cultivated in space?
NATIONAL ARCHIVES/WIKIMEDIA COMMONS/PUBLIC DOMAIN

Sometimes we need to look closely to find the right solutions.
VESNAANDJIC/GETTY IMAGES

Try This! MAKE FOCACCIA FOR DINNER

Eating microbes is not just for astronauts. If you had toast for breakfast or a sandwich for lunch, you've already consumed microbial yeast. In this recipe, you'll see yeast make bread rise by breaking down sugar and producing carbon dioxide.

Ingredients:

- 1 ¾ cups warm water
- 1 tablespoon traditional baking yeast
- 1 teaspoon sugar
- 2 teaspoons salt (plus more for topping)
- ¼ cup olive oil (plus more for topping)
- 4 cups flour

Method:

1. Combine water, yeast and sugar in a large bowl. Watch it foam up! This is evidence of the yeast actively eating the sugar in the water.
2. Stir in salt and olive oil.
3. Add flour, one cup at a time, and stir with wooden spoon.
4. Knead the dough until smooth and elastic (about 10 minutes), sprinkling flour on your counter to stop it from sticking.
5. Put the ball of dough in a bowl that's been lightly coated with oil. Cover with a kitchen cloth and set it in a warm spot for the yeast to work.
6. As the sugar in the flour gets broken down, the ball of dough will become full of carbon dioxide and double in size after about an hour and a half. Punch it down (not too hard!) and let it rise again until doubled in size.
7. Preheat oven to 350 degrees Fahrenheit.
8. Put dough in a well-oiled 12-by-16-inch dish (or baking sheet with half-inch sides). Stretch gently to fit in pan. Drizzle top with olive oil and sprinkle with salt. Using your fingertips, poke little indentations (not holes) over the entire surface.
9. Bake for 20 minutes. Top should be golden when done.

Let your focaccia cool a bit before digging in, but don't be afraid to serve it warm. It's a delicious snack, especially when dipped in olive oil and balsamic vinegar. You could also serve it for dinner with soup or salad or any of your other favorite foods!

What Are Yeasts?

Yeasts are single-celled members of the Fungi kingdom. There are about 1,500 different species of yeast. Selected strains of one yeast species probably helped make the bread in your sandwich.

DR_MICROBE/GETTY IMAGES

MERC67/GETTY IMAGES

Relics found in Egypt that date back to 1353–1336 BCE provide evidence that ancient cultures loved bread as much as we do.
THE METROPOLITAN MUSEUM OF ART/GIFT OF NORBERT SCHIMMEL, 1985/PUBLIC DOMAIN

Fermenting a Miracle

Before fridges, freezers and other clever ways of preserving food, there was *fermentation*. Just as bacteria ferments milk into cheese, different microbes are now being used to produce foods with various textures, flavors and nutritional properties. Because many are high in protein, they are often made into fillets, burgers, sausages and nuggets as alternatives to meat.

These modern foods might be the solution to feeding our growing planet in the future, but fermentation has been around for centuries. The earliest historical record comes from Egypt over 5,000 years ago, when someone figured out that leaving a mixture of flour and water to sit in a warm place before baking produced a lighter and tastier loaf of bread. Because they didn't know about yeast and fermentation, it was considered a miracle.

Fermented fungi spores are used to create mycoprotein, an ingredient found in some meat alternatives.
DANIEL NEVILLE/WIKIMEDIA COMMONS/CC BY-SA 2.0

CHAPTER FOUR

Energizing Earth

Power plants that burn fossil fuels such as coal release a lot of carbon dioxide into the atmosphere.
NIRUTISTOCK/GETTY IMAGES

There are many different types of pollution, and they're all bad. But the one we'll focus on in this final chapter has contributed to what's now considered a worldwide crisis: carbon dioxide.

Earth's atmosphere has always contained some carbon dioxide. Like a soil microbiome—and many other things in nature—the amount of carbon dioxide must be balanced with other gases like nitrogen and oxygen for the world to be healthy.

Climate naturally changes over long periods of time, but right now our climate is changing very quickly because of an imbalance caused by human activities such as burning fossil fuels for energy. Too much carbon dioxide in the atmosphere creates what's known as the greenhouse effect—the carbon dioxide traps heat near the planet's surface. As a result, global temperatures are on the rise, as are sea levels, and we're experiencing weather extremes and natural disasters like wildfires and storms.

Microbes can help us deal with the climate crisis in two different ways: by helping us capture some of the carbon dioxide in the air, and by providing a source of energy to replace fossil fuels.

CARBON CAPTURE

You're probably already familiar with one form of carbon capture—you may have even planted a seed and helped capture some carbon yourself. In the same way we breathe in oxygen and breathe out carbon dioxide, plants breathe in carbon dioxide and breathe out oxygen. Through photosynthesis—a process of converting sunlight into sugar—plants suck carbon dioxide out of the air and use it to grow.

Once carbon has been captured from the air, plants store it in their leaves, branches, stems and roots. When a tree grows very big, it's capturing and storing a lot of carbon. When a tree dies, or a leaf falls, this locked-up carbon enters the ground and is stored there. What can we do to conserve this natural cycle? First, we need to manage forests so fires don't get out of control, because when trees burn, carbon is released back into the atmosphere. Second, we must cut down fewer trees to grow crops or build factories. Third, we can support plant growth by protecting their biggest supporters—soil microbes.

Microbes help trees capture carbon dioxide and store it. When trees burn, carbon dioxide is released.
MLHARING/GETTY IMAGES

We work hard to keep our gardens healthy—and so do microbes!
KRYZHOV/SHUTTERSTOCK.COM

Mycorrhizal networks below the ground are often bigger than the trees that grow from them.
ORLA/GETTY IMAGES

Mycorrhizal Networks

We're back to *myco*, the prefix mushroom scientists love so much. This time it's being used to describe mycelium that create underground networks connecting one tree's roots to another's. Like we use the fiber optics of an internet network to exchange information, trees use mycorrhizal networks to exchange water and valuable nutrients with one another. As part of this symbiotic relationship, trees give fungi carbon and sugars for their own growth. (Just like us, trees need a reliable network!)

Plants aren't the only living things made of carbon. Animals are partly made of carbon too, including you and me! Almost one-fifth of the human body is carbon (18 percent of our weight). So it's probably not surprising that fungi contain carbon too.

To figure out how much of the world's carbon is stored in mycorrhizal networks, a team of scientists from South Africa, the Netherlands, United States and Belgium collected information from past research studies. The number they came up with is over 11.5 billion tons (13 billion metric tons). That's huge! It means the network of microbes beneath our feet (not just under forests, parks and grassland but roads, gardens and houses as well) holds as much as one-third (36 percent) of the world's yearly carbon production from fossil-fuel emissions.

Imagine if all that carbon remained in the atmosphere. Given how much the current climate crisis is already affecting our lives, it's probably not something you want to think about. But it shows how important it is to protect the hardworking microbes beneath the ground and not just the trees and plants we see above it.

Algae Meets AI

Okay, so plants and mycorrhizal networks do a great job of storing carbon under the ground. But only about a third of Earth is covered in land. What about the other 70 percent of the planet? Oceans also absorb a lot of carbon dioxide through vegetation, coral and…algae. Like plants, algae take carbon dioxide from the air and use it to grow more algae.

When you put a single tree into battle against algae, there's no doubt the tree will be able to capture and store more carbon. But if we allow for teamwork, algae have a few big advantages:

1. They grow fast.
2. They don't take up much space (no forest or farm required!).
3. They can grow in extreme conditions, including high temperatures.

Why am I making this into a competition? Because scientists have shown that algae can be up to 400 times more efficient than a tree at removing carbon dioxide from the atmosphere when grown in bioreactors using **artificial intelligence** (AI). There are two really cool aspects to this technology. One is the AI (of course!), which is a continuous monitoring system that adjusts things like light and temperature as well as the balance of gas in the air and minerals in the water to optimize algae growth. The second is the bioreactors, which can be made in any size or shape, from a small, decorative container that sits

How Small Do They Get?

Picoplankton, the smallest algae known, is only 0.000008 inches (200 nanometers) or less in diameter. The prefix *nano* (one-billionth) is used to describe a lot of tiny things, but *pico* (one-trillionth) is even more microscopic. Fungi can be just as pico-sized, with over seven miles (11 kilometers) of mycorrhizal network fungi tubes in just one pinch of soil!

With the help of AI, bioreactors are designed to grow algae as efficiently as possible.
SANTIAGO URQUIJO/GETTY IMAGES

on your kitchen counter to a large unit hooked up directly to a factory's exhaust pipe—vacuuming up carbon to feed the algae inside before it even hits the air!

MIGHTY MICROBES

Now the question is, what do we do with all the algae grown in these bioreactors? The answer could be a solution to decreasing the use of fossil fuels for energy so we can reduce carbon dioxide emissions. It's generally understood that we need to start using more renewable sources of power, like sun, wind and water. But it turns out there is another option too. All three of the microbes we've talked about in this book—bacteria, fungi and algae—can be used as fuel to create energy as well.

Algae Fuel

The bioreactors we talked about in the last section create blocks of algae that are described as "carbon hockey pucks" by the AI company developing the technology. They say the pucks can be used for everything from fuel to the bioplastics discussed in chapter 2 (but probably not for playing hockey).

Another team has taken algae growth out of the bioreactor and back to the pond. With help from AI, they broke a world record by producing 1.4 ounces (43.3 grams) of algae per 10 square feet (1 square meter) per day. That's about two AA batteries in weight on an area half the size of your bed. It might not sound like a lot, but remember, these are microorganisms grown to a size you can not only see but hold in your hand—in just one day! They also found a more efficient way to harvest the algae, making it cheaper than other algae-based fuels. Researchers hope these record-breaking algae can be turned into a less-polluting form of fuel for airplanes.

Algae fuel isn't just green in color—it's friendly to the environment too.
(MAIN) SCHARFSINN86/GETTY IMAGES;
(INSET) ASHLEY COOPER/GETTY IMAGES

Electromicrobiology

Since algae has some of the same compounds found in petroleum—one of the reasons it's a good substitute for petroplastic, as we discussed in chapter 2—it's probably not a stretch to think of it as a type of gasoline. And it's not the only microbe made up of compounds similar to fuels we already use. There's even a poisonous mushroom that contains a toxin used in rocket fuel!

There's a bug hiding out in certain soils, though, that could revolutionize the way we think about energy production. *Geobacter,* a type of bacteria, has caught the attention of scientists because of a unique superpower—it eats chemicals and poops out electricity! No, it doesn't have a microbutt. But it does push out energy by transferring "waste" away from its body through tiny hairs referred to as nanowires.

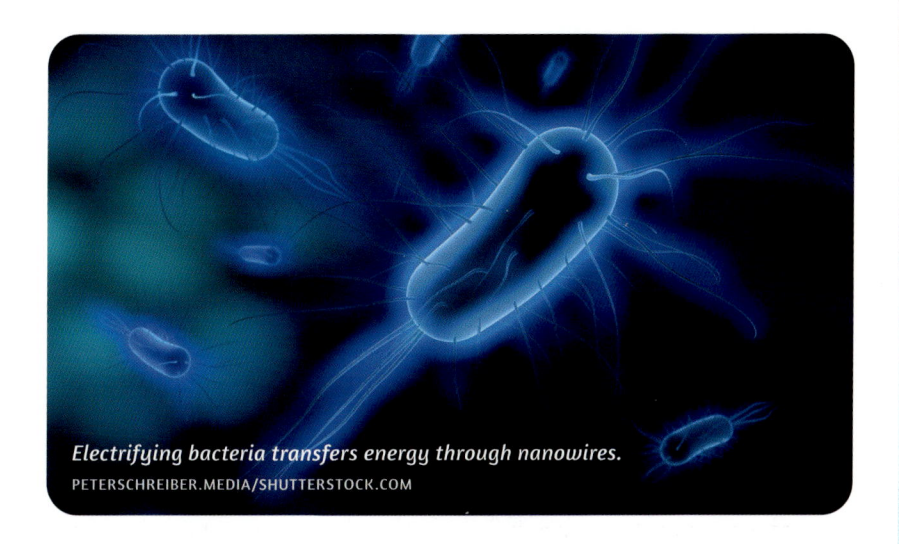

Electrifying bacteria transfers energy through nanowires.
PETERSCHREIBER.MEDIA/SHUTTERSTOCK.COM

Through these nanowires, *Geobacter* produces electric currents that deliver energy to minerals in the environment. What if we could capture that power in a battery that could be used in everything from phones to cars? Or maybe put the bacteria directly into electronic devices so we could plug them into a jar of chemical compounds instead of a wall outlet?

How Big Do They Get?

Some algae and fungi get so big, it's hard to believe they're related to microbes. Kelp is a kind of algae that can grow as long as 200 feet (60 meters), which is as long as an NHL ice rink. But that's nothing compared to a honey mushroom found growing in the Blue Mountains of Oregon. Considered the largest organism on Earth, it's nearly 4 square miles (10 square kilometers) in size—big enough to cover almost 1,665 football fields! No wonder it earned the nickname "humongous fungus."

Soil or Dirt?

Many of us think of soil and dirt as the same thing. But soil's actually a type of dirt—the type that contains microbes!

There's no single way to save the planet, but microbes could be the answer to cleaning up some of the messes we've made.
HRYSHCHYSHEN SERHII/SHUTTERSTOCK.COM

It might even be possible to isolate nanowires and sandwich them in a way that creates energy through a circuit—out of nothing but air!

As research into these possibilities continues, a new field of electromicrobiology has emerged. It turns out that *Geobacter* isn't the only electrifying bacteria. But *Geobacter* is a bug with more than one superpower. It can also feast off toxic metals and sponge up oil pollution, just like the mycelium you read about at the beginning of the book.

The Microbial Revolution

Whether we use the oily component of microalgae to make biofuel or bacteria to create electricity, many microbiologists believe that microbes could provide another alternative to fossil fuels. One day your jeans could be made in a factory powered by microbes. Or maybe they'll be made of microbes! Are both these possibilities—and more—part of an upcoming microbial revolution? The answer may be too small to see, but thanks to microbes, there's hope for a cleaner future on planet Earth.

Under the Microscope
Too Good to Be True?

When we look for new and inventive ways to both clean up pollution and produce less of it, we need to make sure we're not creating new problems at the same time. This is especially true with regard to carbon storage and alternative fuels.

Because human activity has put so much carbon dioxide in the air, mycorrhizal networks and algae are having a tough time keeping up, especially as we continue to pollute both the soil and water they live in. One way of helping involves pumping carbon dioxide directly into the ground ourselves. The question is, what happens to the carbon dioxide after it's been tucked away? Can it escape? Does it get transformed into something else? Something worse? Since microbes are everywhere—breaking down matter and converting it into something different—they may be part of the answer to all these questions.

As a group, biofuels emit less carbon dioxide into the environment than fossil fuels. But we need to make sure that the process of making biofuels is energy efficient and doesn't produce pollution such as carbon dioxide or, again, something even worse.

Microbes are an important part of every ecosystem. Understanding their role and protecting their diversity are vital to the health of both people and the planet.
(MAIN) GORODENKOFF/GETTY IMAGES; (INSET) JOYIMAGE/GETTY IMAGES

TOUGH DECISIONS AHEAD

Try This! CREATE AN ALGAE BIOREACTOR

Ready to try to beat AI? In this experiment, you'll design your own bioreactor to optimize algae growth.

Materials:

- Three (or more) glass jars (recycled plastic bottles also work)
- Pond water (or other source of algae, such as marsh, swamp, swimming pool, fish aquarium, bird bath)
- Liquid plant food (available at garden stores—10-15-10 is ideal)
- Optional additives: laundry detergent, dishwasher detergent, vinegar, fertilizers

Method:

1. Fill bottles with pond water, being sure to include any visible algae.
2. Add liquid plant food to all bottles. If you can't find liquid plant food that's okay, it just means the algae will grow more slowly.
3. If using detergents or vinegar, add one thing to each bottle, making sure to label what you've added. Place all jars in a warm, sunny spot and monitor algae growth.
4. If not using additives, place each jar in a different location around the house. Each spot should have a different environmental condition. Put one in direct sunlight and one in the shade, for example.

Be experimental! You may find that certain detergents make algae grow quicker and others make them grow slower. Look at the ingredients in the detergent itself to figure out what the magic formula is (hint: phosphorus helps!). Warmth and sunlight also make a big difference.

Take your bioreactor to the next level by supplying your algae with carbon dioxide. To do this, add 2 teaspoons of sugar and 1 teaspoon of brewer's yeast to another jar half-full of purified water (all these ingredients should be available at the supermarket or grocery store). Take a flexible piece of tubing (find this at pet stores that sell aquarium equipment or use a long straw) and tape one end to the side of the jar so the opening is above the water. Seal the top around the tubing with plastic wrap or foil. Submerge the other end of the tube in the pond water to deliver the carbon dioxide produced from the yeast and sugar to your algae.

KIRSTY BEGG/STOCKSY.COM

Acknowledgments

All books are hard to write (for me, anyway!), but this book about small things was especially challenging because the topic is so big! Microbes really are vital to life on Earth, and there are so many examples of how they can help us deal with pollution and the climate crisis. Reading about all the research being done to promote, protect and perfect microbes was fascinating.

I couldn't have done all the necessary research and writing (and rewriting) without the Creative Writers grant I received from the BC Arts Council. I'm grateful to live in a province and country that supports artists and creators. I recognize that I'm a guest in the traditional territory of the Sinixt Nation and that I'm privileged to work, live and play on Indigenous land.

Huge thanks to my friends and family, especially Spencer, Oliver and Tim (who patiently listened to my latest microbe discovery over many family dinners). Thank you also to Orca—I love being part of the pod—as well as the teachers, librarians and booksellers who help kids get access to books they both love and learn from. And, finally, a heartfelt thanks to you, the reader. Thank you for giving me the opportunity to share my passion for writing and the natural world.

Resources

Print

Alexander, Lori, and Vivien Mildenberger. *All in a Drop: How Antony van Leeuwenhoek Discovered an Invisible World.* Clarion Books, 2019.

Ferron, Sheddad Kaid-Salah, and Eduard Altarriba. *My First Book of Microbes: Viruses, Bacteria, Fungi, and More.* Button Books, 2022.

Mould, Steve. *The Bacteria Book: The Big World of Really Tiny Microbes.* DK Children, 2018.

Rajcak, Hélène, and Damien Laverdunt. *Unseen Worlds: Real-Life Microscopic Creatures Hiding All Around Us.* What on Earth Books, 2019.

Wohlleben, Peter, and Shelley Tanaka. *Can You Hear the Trees Talking? Discovering the Hidden Life of the Forest.* Greystone Kids, 2019.

Online

American Museum of Natural History, "Ology": amnh.org/explore/ology/microbiology

Growing Play, "Soil Facts for Kids": growingplay.com/2022/04/soil-facts-for-kids

Let's Talk Science, "Are Microbes Your Friend or Foe?": letstalkscience.ca/educational-resources/stem-explained/are-microbes-your-friend-or-foe

North American Mycological Association, "The Fungus Files": namyco.org/fungus_files.php

Links to external resources are for personal and/or educational use only and are provided in good faith without any express or implied warranty. There is no guarantee given as to the accuracy or currency of any individual item. The author and publisher provide links as a service to readers. This does not imply any endorsement by the author or publisher of any of the content accessed through these links.

Glossary

3D printing—a method of building a solid three-dimensional object layer by layer using a computer-created design

artificial intelligence—the ability of a computer to think and learn

biodegradable—can be broken down or decomposed by living organisms such as microbes

bioreactors—containers in which raw materials are converted into something else by living organisms such as microbes

carbon—a natural element found in all forms of life

carbon dioxide—a gas with no color or smell that's produced by respiration and by burning carbon

cell—the smallest biological unit of all living things

climate crisis—term used in an article signed by over 11,000 scientists worldwide to describe the global threat posed by rapid changes to Earth's climate system, which are currently causing an overall rise in temperature and increased extreme weather events across the planet

ecosystem—a complex system in which everything that exists in a particular environment, including plants, animals, rocks, weather, soil, water, sunlight, etc., relies on the other parts of the environment in the same way

enzyme—a substance made by the cells of plants and animals that creates and controls chemical reactions

evolve—develop over generations through changes to the genome

fermentation—a natural process through which starches and sugars are converted into a new product by microbes

fertilizers—substances added to soil or sprayed on plant leaves to help crops grow better

fossil fuels—the remains of dead plants and animals that are extracted from below Earth's crust, processed into crude oil, natural gas or coal and burned to create energy

gene editing—inserting, removing or changing the genome to make specific changes in an organism

genome—genetic material containing all the information an organism needs to develop and grow

invasive species—any species of plant, animal, fungus or bacterium that causes harm when introduced to a new habitat, where it has no natural enemies and therefore can reproduce and spread unchecked

microbiome—a microbial community that lives in animal bodies, plants, land and oceans

mycoremediation—the process of bringing something back to a desirable state using fungi

nuclear power plants—power stations where the smallest units of matter are split apart in reactors to produce energy

organic matter—material that comes from a living organism and is capable of or the product of decay

organism—a living thing that grows, reproduces and reacts to other living and nonliving things in the environment

pesticides—substances used to control or kill pests like weeds and insects

petroleum—a fossil fuel used to make gasoline

photosynthesis—the process of converting sunlight, water and carbon dioxide into oxygen and energy in the form of sugar

pollution—something that harms the environment when it's released into the air, water or land

radiation—energy that moves from one place to another in the form of waves or particle streams

symbiotic—involving an interaction between two different organisms in which each provides the other with the conditions necessary for survival

synthetic—not found in nature, or human-made

Index

*Page numbers in **bold** indicate an image caption.*

3D printing, 23, 49

agriculture: diet changes, 31–35; farm-free food, 7, 32–34; food production, 26–30; hydroponics, **26**; land use, 32, 33; and runoff, 8–9, 11, 24, 26; three sisters planting, 29
algae: about, 9, 43; and bioplastics, 21, 22–24; blooms, 24; blue-green, 33; and carbon capture, 41; defined, 21; downside of use, 24; kelp, 23, 43; picoplankton, 41; seaweed, 22–23
algae-based fuels, 42–43, 44
algae bioreactor experiment, 46
Amazon Mycorenewal Project, 12–13
artificial intelligence (AI), 41, 49
astronauts, food in space, 15, 32, 33, **34**
aviation fuels, 42

bacteria: about, 9, 20, 31; defined, 19; isolating enzyme in, 20; nitrogen-fixing, 29; plastic-eating, 7, 19–20
bacteria-based energy, 43–44
bacterial colony, **20**
biodegradable, 18, 23, 24, 49
biofoam products, 23
biofuels, 42–43, 44, 45
bioplastics, 22–24
bioreactors: and algae growth, 41–42; bioplastics, 23; defined, 49; experiment, 46; microbial proteins, 32, 34
breads, 36, 37

carbon, 40–41, 49
carbon capture: and bioplastics, 22; defined, 39; downside of use, 45; and microbes, 7, 38–41

carbon dioxide, 22, 45, 49
carrots, growing, **28**
cells, 23, 34, 49
chemicals, toxic, 11–13, 18, 24, 44
Cheng, Liang, 30
Chernobyl nuclear disaster, 14–15
climate crisis: and algae, 22–24; carbon dioxide levels, 13; causes, 38; defined, 49; and diet changes, 31–35; innovations, 11, 22–23, 33, 41–42; sustainable farming, 26–30; yearly emissions, 40; *See also* solutions
clothing, 8, 11
composting, 18, 25
consumers: clothing, 8, 11; and diet changes, 31–35; microbial proteins, 32–34; packaging, 22–23
corn, 26, 29
cotton, 8, **9**, 11, 18

deforestation, 39

ecosystems, 7, 15, 21, 28, 49
Ecuador, oil spill, 12–13
Egypt, ancient, 37
electromicrobiology, 43–44
energy sources: bacteria-based, 43–44; biofuels, 42–43, 44, 45; fossil fuels, 18, 21, 24, 38, 49; nuclear, 12, 14–15, 50; renewable energy, 12, 42
enzyme action, 20, 24, 49
evolve/evolution, 20, 49

farm-free food: hydroponics, **26**; microbial proteins, 32–34
fashion industry, 8, 11

fermentation, 37, 49
fertilizers, 8, 11, 24, 26, 28, 49
focaccia bread recipe, 36
food containers, compostable, **22**, 23
food production: gene editing, 34, 49; microbial proteins, 32–34, 37; *See also* agriculture
forest fires, **39**
fossil fuels: and climate crisis, 38; defined, 49; oil spills, 12–13; petroplastics, 18, 21, 24
fuel sources. *See* energy sources
fungi: about, 9, 10, 43; downside of use, 15; and ionizing radiation, 14–15; mushrooms, 10, 15, 16–17, 43; mycelium, 10–15, 40–41; mycoremediation, 10–15, 50; mycorrhizal networks, 40–41; yeasts, 10, 32, 36, 37

gene editing, 34, 49
genome, 20, 34, 49
Geobacter (bacteria), 43–44

Hoitink, Aniela, 11
human health: digestion, 28; illness, 19, **31**

Indigenous community: Amazon River, 12–13; knowledge, 29
invasive species, 15, 34, 50

kelp, 23, 43

meat alternatives, 32–34, 37
melanin, 14–15, 20
Melvin, Leland, **34**
metals, toxic, 11, 44

51

Index (continued)

methane gas, **27**
microbial proteins, 32–34, 37
microbes: about, 7, 9, 31; carbon capture, 38–41; decomposing of, 18; defined, 6; and digestive process, **27**, 28; and farming, 27–30; and food revolution, 32–34; as fuel, 42–43, 44, 45; and mycelium, 10–15, 40–41
microbiomes, 28–30, 50, 54
microplastics, 22
mushrooms: about, 10, 15; as fuels, 43; growing, 16–17; honey, 43; *See also* fungi
mycelium: defined, 10; mycorrhizal networks, 40–41; reversing environmental damage, 10–15
mycoprotein, 37
mycoremediation, 10–15, 50
mycorrhizal networks, 40–41
MycoTex, 11

New Zealand, oil spill, **12**
nitrogen-fixing bacteria, 29
nuclear power plants, 12, 14–15, 50

oceans: and carbon capture, 41; cleanup, 11, **12**, 24
oil companies, 12–13
organic matter: biodegradable, 18, 23, 24, 50; and fungi, 10
organisms, 6, 50
Oyster mushrooms, 16–17

packaging, compostable, 7, 22–23
pesticides, 8, 11, 26, 28, 50
petroleum: defined, 50; petroplastics, 18, 21, 24; *See also* fossil fuels
photosynthesis, 10, 21, 39, 50

picoplankton, 41
plants: and carbon capture, 39; mycorrhizal networks, 40–41; roots, **28**, **29**; symbiotic, 29, 40, 50
plastics: bioplastics, 21, 22–24; breakdown of, 19–20; common uses, 20; petroplastics, 18; polymers, 21–22, 23
pollution: defined, 50; and food production, 8–9, 11, 24, 26; plastics, 18–24; solutions, 7, 45; sources of, 8–9, 22, 38; *See also* toxic materials
pond scum, 21, 32, 33
power plants, **38**
projects: algae bioreactor experiment, 46; focaccia bread recipe, 36; microcomposter, 25; mushroom growing, 16–17
protein, alternative, 32–34, 37
protein powder, 32

radiation, 14–15, 50
resources, 48

seaweed, 22–23
soil: and composting, 18, 25; healthy, 27–30, 39, **44**; microbiomes, 28–30, 50, 54
solutions: biofuels, 42–43, 44, 45; microbial proteins, 32–34; renewable energy, 12, 42; research, 28, 30, **35**, 42, **45**
space travel, food sources, 15, 32, 33, **34**
spirulina (supplement), 33
sustainable future. *See* solutions
symbiotic, 29, 40, 50
synthetic, 11, 26, 50

technology: artificial intelligence (AI), 41, 49; bioplastics, 22–24; bioreactors, 23, 32, 34, 49; gene editing, 34, 49; microbial proteins, 32–34; radiation protection, 15; weed control, 30
toxic materials: air pollution, 38; algae blooms, 24; breakdown of, **12**, 13, 18; radiation, 14–15; removal, 11, 44

Ukraine, Chernobyl disaster, 14–15

Vague, Morgan, 19, 20

yeasts, 10, 32, 36, 37